• Minehead • Dunster • Blue Anchor • Washford • Wa
Heathfield • Crowcombe Heathfield • Bi

WEST SOMERSET RAILWAY

GUIDE BOOK

Right: North Hill dominates the skyline of Minehead, representing the point where Exmoor comes down to the Bristol Channel, with the town extending part way up its slopes. The modernistic pavilion building is part of the Butlins Holiday Centre from where many holidaymakers come to enjoy a day out on the railway and in the surrounding area. *Don Bishop*

Welcome

The West Somerset Railway is Britain's longest standard gauge heritage railway and carries more than 200,000 passengers per year, making it one of Somerset's most popular tourist attractions. Passenger trains run during most months of the year, with services from early February to early December. In addition to offering an 80-minute 'pink knuckle' ride through the Quantock Hills and along the Exmoor Coast, the railway has also developed a number of combined packages with other local attractions including Dunster Castle and Hestercombe Gardens, as well as day trips across Exmoor and exploring the remains of the old West Somerset Mineral Railway. Much more information can be obtained by ringing 01643 704996 or viewing the Company website at:
www.west-somerset-railway.co.uk.

An outline history of the West Somerset Line

Railways in the nineteenth century were usually promoted by enterprising local businessmen who saw an opportunity to increase their trade by improving communications and the original West Somerset Railway was an example of the breed. It was born of the desire of the old harbour own of Watchet to gain a link to the developing national railway network which already saw rival Bristol Channel ports such as Highbridge, Dunball and Bridgwater feeling the benefits of their connections to the Bristol and Exeter Railway which had been engineered by Brunel and was part of a route that linked London and Cornwall.

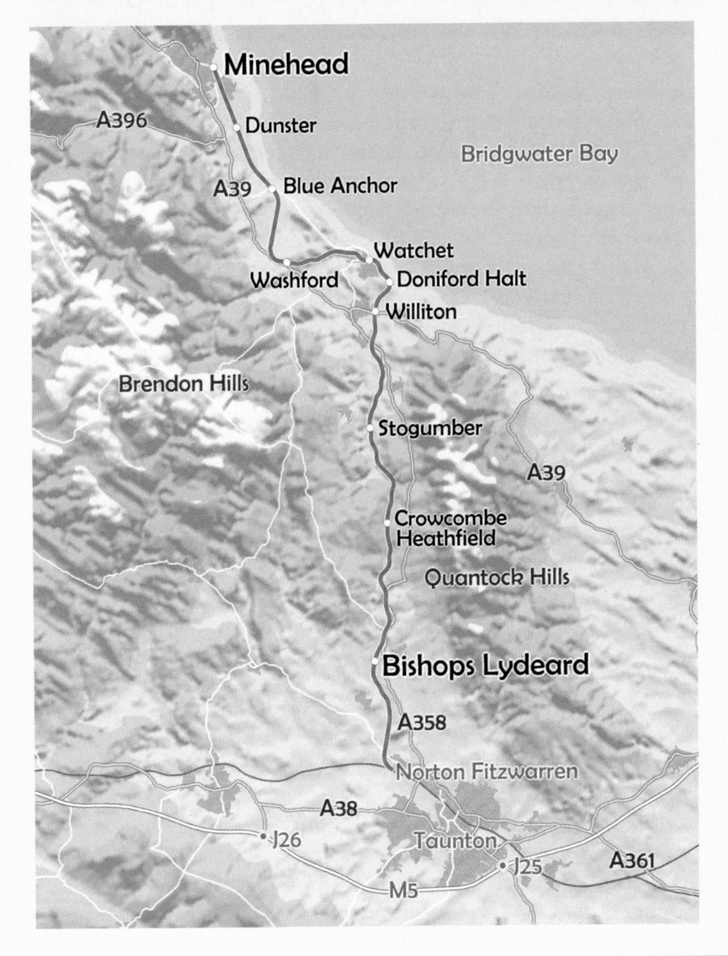

Above: Locomotive No 9351 is an interesting WSR creation, a steam locomotive designed by the Great Western Railway in the 1930s but not actually built by the GWR. The West Somerset converted scrap-condition 'Large Prairie' tank engine No 5193 to produce this 'Small Boilered Mogul', and seven decades after the original design it has proved to be an excellent engine. *Don Bishop*

Great Western 'auto-trains' never operated on the Minehead line in GWR or British Railways days, being deployed on less heavily used branch lines, but they have proved very popular attractions during Enthusiast Gala events. *WSR Collection*

Watchet had actually heard its first steam engines at work in 1856 when the West Somerset Mineral Railway was built. However as the name suggests this was built for a specific purpose, that of bringing down iron ore from mines in the Brendon Hills to the harbour for shipping to the furnaces in Ebbw Vale in South Wales. The Mineral Line was an interesting piece of engineering including a large and steeply graded cable worked incline at Comberrow but it went inland and although it ran passenger services through villages such as Washford and Roadwater it was not capable of becoming the larger commercial route Watchet needed. Dependent for most of its traffic on the mines the WSMR declined as cheaper and better quality ores were brought in from Spain and despite an attempted revival at the start of the 20th Century its rails were torn up in 1917. Today various remains can be found and the route between Watchet and Washford is a popular footpath.

Having decided to build a new line towards the Bristol and Exeter where it passed through the county town of Somerset at Taunton the local backers of the scheme sought an engineer for the construction and engaged no less a figure than Isambard Kingdom Brunel. In the 19th century engineers could attain what today would be regarded as "celebrity" status – although it can easily be argued on much firmer ground than most of the "celebs" two centuries on – and Brunel had a high reputation in South West England despite the debacle of the South Devon Railway's atmospheric railway working system which cost a lot of South Devon investors a great deal of money before the idea of working trains by creating a vacuum ahead of them was abandoned in favour of orthodox operation by steam locomotives.

Brunel accepted the title but in fact the practical work of building the line was supervised by two of his assistants, Mr. Burke and Mr. Brereton. The great man was fully occupied with work on the bridge at Saltash which was to get the railways into Cornwall and the steamship the "Great Eastern", being built at Millwall. Constructing what was essentially a branch line was by the 1850s a fairly routine procedure and a survey showed that to

Class 158 diesel units would be ideal candidates for any regular services between the main-line network and Minehead if these were to come about. In the meantime they sometimes appear at Bishops Lydeard on shuttles from Taunton during special events.
Claire Rickson

Time Line

1856-1862
West Somerset Railway constructed between Norton Fitzwarren and Watchet
1874
Line extended to Minehead
1882
Line converted from broad gauge to standard gauge
1934
Final expansion occurs
1948
Railways nationalised
1971
Minehead branch closed by British Rail
1976
First WSR trains begin running between Minehead and Blue Anchor
1979
Train operations reach full length of line between Minehead and Bishops Lydeard
2012
150th Anniversary

get through the Quantock Hills a water course could be followed to the summit and another back to the level ground between Williton and Watchet. After that there was the usual battle to obtain land with a hapless valuer stuck between what the local land owners wanted and what the Directors, as guided by the engineers, were prepared to pay. Brunel is recorded as having attended some of the board meetings (which were held in Taunton or at the now-closed Egremont Hotel in Williton) including one where curiously he is in the record books (which can be found in National Archive at Kew) as having been present but did not speak. In 1859 Brunel was felled by a fatal stroke, brought on by a life of constant over-working, but the line was opened from Watchet to a junction at Norton Fitzwarren some two and half miles from Taunton. Construction had begun at the highest point of the line, near what became Crowcombe Heathfield station, a traditional process that allowed material excavated from cuttings to be used for construction of embankments, and then progressed to Watchet and the junction with the Bristol and Exeter Railway's main line at Norton Fitzwarren, west of Taunton.

As a Brunel line it was built to his broad gauge of seven feet and a quarter inch and was effectively worked as part of the Bristol and Exeter Railway from the start.

In 1874 a nominally separate

Enthusiast Galas bring large numbers of passengers, photographers and visitors to the WSR, and here a demonstration 'heritage' freight train passes a shuttle-service Class 158 unit at Bishops Lydeard station. *Claire Rickson*

company, the Minehead Railway, was promoted to extend the existing line from Watchet through Washford and Dunster to a small town that was then being developed as a seaside resort. Minehead had had a long history as a port town but it had never been as prosperous as Watchet (there had also been a harbour on the flat ground below Dunster but this had silted up and ceased to exist. Today the site can be found as a shallow depression near to the Dunster Beach Holidays site). However, with the growth in seaside holidays local landowners could see the potential for establishing a new resort on the Bristol Channel Coast and a railway could augment the ships in the Bristol Channel to bring in the guests to the new hotels and guest houses.

The Minehead Railway was also built to the broad gauge but with most of Britain's network having been built to the Stephenson standard gauge of four feet eight and a half inches Brunel's vision was eventually doomed and in 1882 the whole line from Norton Fitzwarren to Minehead was converted to the main-line standard (in 24 hours from start to finish) which did mean that goods could travel nationwide without having to be transferred from one train to another at the breaks of gauge.

As the 19th century turned into the 20th passenger traffic grew on the line and alterations were made to the stations, particularly the length of the platforms which were extended to cope with the longer trains and the larger locomotives which were used to haul them. The final development in this field was in 1934 and it is most noticeable when entering the station at Minehead and noting the distance to the signal box or at Washford when looking towards Minehead from the station building. Other key developments were the installation of passing loops and new platforms at Bishops Lydeard, Crowcombe Heathfield and Blue Anchor Stations, and also between stations at Leigh Woods (between Crowcombe Heathfield

'The Beeching axe'

When in 1962 Dr Richard Beeching produced his report 'The Reshaping of British Railways', the Minehead line was earmarked for closure.

It was, however, a marginal case. Whereas the other branch lines from Taunton to Chard (closed 1962), Yeovil (closed 1964) and Barnstaple (closed 1966) went fairly quickly, the Minehead made money in the summer and lost it in the winter.

and Stogumber) and Kentsford (between Watchet and Washford).

The final boom years were the 1950s and the early 60s as wartime austerity wore off and the British people resumed the habit of seaside holidays and day trips. On summer Saturdays branch lines throughout the South West of England were worked to capacity and beyond with staff working many hours of overtime to cope with the number of passengers and their luggage. In the case of the Minehead line this was compounded when Butlins opened one of their holiday camps. However, the trains carrying these crowds were often made up of stock that only worked on these weekends and were otherwise parked up in sidings and these older carriages were too often without corridors or toilets. After spending a number of hours travelling in those conditions in crowded (and often delayed) trains it was no surprise that when the passengers got home they went to the car showrooms and talked hire purchase terms or began to look at the brochures from the road coach companies.

Alongside this part of the story local traffic had begun a decline in the 1920s as ex-army vehicles surplus after World War I became available for the start of lorry haulage businesses or conversion to buses. As they became more reliable and rural buses became more comfortable their door-to-door potential began to erode the attraction of walking to the local station. On the Minehead line this becomes obvious at locations like Crowcombe Heathfield, Stogumber or Dunster. What is a pleasant stroll to and from the village on a summer's day was less fun on a day-in-day-out basis in the winter months and these were far from being the most spectacular examples. If the Great Western put the word "Road" after a village name there would be a walk of considerably more than a mile to be tackled and often the community "served" might not be in sight from the station platform.

So as the 1960s progressed more branch lines began to close and the rate quickened enormously after Dr Richard Beeching published his report "The Reshaping of British Railways". Of the four local lines which once ran from Taunton the one to Chard closed in 1962, Yeovil went in 1964 and the long route to Barnstaple in 1966.

The Minehead branch was a marginal case. It was essentially profitable in the summer but lost money heavily in the winter and when in 1970 Somerset County Council moved the last of the school traffic to the roads it marked the end. Freight traffic had already ceased and the last passenger trains ran at the start of January 1971.

In the normal run of things this would have been followed by the removal of the track and as the years progressed the removal of the bridges, demolition or conversion of buildings and the general disappearance of the line. But there were already plans to revive it.

This took the form of another group of local businessmen and enthusiasts who envisaged operating the line as a diesel-worked commuter line all year round with seasonal steam trains in the tourist season. With this scheme in mind the County Council stepped in to secure the land and what of the railway's infrastructure had survived being run-down in the 1960s, and a growing number of volunteers began the work of painting, weeding and rebuilding. Even then it took five years

Taunton – so near and yet so far...

The eventual target was to run commuter trains to Taunton, but now a major problem emerged.

When bus services were being introduced in the West of England, many were originally operated by the Great Western Railway, and a legacy of this was that many drivers employed by the Western National company were members of the National Union of Railwaymen, and the WSR trains were viewed as potentially taking business from the then route 218 between Taunton and Minehead. The junction at Norton Fitzwarren and access to Taunton station were 'blacked', and the existing year-round West Somerset trains were confined to running through the smaller towns and villages along the way. Reduced-price travel was available for local residents, but even so usage of winter trains fell away, with the county town and its station being so near and yet so far.

before the first train, steam worked, left Minehead for a round trip to Blue Anchor on Good Friday 1976. Over the next three years there was a steady extension of the length of operations until in 1979 trains were running between Minehead and Bishops Lydeard, some four miles from Taunton. It was an impressive feat but the proverbial storm clouds were gathering.

Firstly, as a result of the way that public transport had developed in the South West the local bus drivers were members of the National Union of Railwaymen and when the prospect of trains returning to the Minehead-Taunton route drew near the NUR decided to protect the bus services by "blacking" the junction at Norton Fitzwarren. Meanwhile the WSR was running a year-round local train service which after a promising start was proving less popular and that situation was compounded further by growing reliability problems with the diesel railcars. In addition the two steam engines which were used at this stage were heavy duty industrial shunting locos which had great reserves of shorter-term power but weren't really suitable for 40-mile round trips over a line with heavy gradients to be climbed. Timekeeping suffered, breakdowns occurred and after spending time on platforms for trains that were either late or didn't turn up at all the locals returned to the buses. By the start of 1981 the situation was grim and closure seemed likely. It was also during this period that as part of re-signalling work at Taunton the up relief line which gave separate access into Taunton station from the main-line junction was taken up and new signalling equipment put in place where it had been, thereby effectively cutting off Taunton for regular WSR trains.

'Will Something Run?'

The steam services depended largely in the early years on two industrial engines, *Victor* and *Vulcan*. Built by Bagnall of Stafford for steelworks use in Wales, they had subsequently gone to Austin Motors at Longbridge, from where they were purchased by the infant WSR. As supremely powerful industrial shunters they may well have been suited to short steam trips for holidaymakers, but a 40-mile round trip with hard climbing and a route that twisted and turned through the hills was not their forte. Timekeeping and reliability was poor, and as the second-hand diesel railcars also suffered from the high mileage, service reliability plummeted to the point where a local joke held that WSR stood for 'Will Something Run?'. To this must be added a complicated early timetable leaflet, which the public found hard to understand.

However, a fight back began. It was painful to start with as nearly all of the paid staff were made redundant (many stayed on as volunteers) and train operating days reduced to times suitable for the leisure industry. The new policy also saw steam trains for this market as the way forward. Slowly the corner was turned and more suitable steam engines began to enter service, either restored to working order on the line or hired in. By the late 1980s things were on a sound footing and a successful share appeal allowed the WSR plc to take a 99-year lease on the line from Somerset County Council, who had been enormously helpful during the darkest period, recognising the potential benefits of a successful steam railway for the local economy.

As passenger numbers and revenues grew it allowed much-needed work to be carried out to restore features which had been lost during the period when BR were running down the facilities in the 1960's. The signalling and passing loop were reinstated at Crowcombe Heathfield, Bishops Lydeard was resignalled and there very many less obvious projects brought to fruition, often funded and carried out by station volunteers. Another major step forward was a long contract when the railway was used to bring rock armour and other large components for sea defence work at Minehead. This was done with main-line trains working from the quarries in the Mendip Hills, running over the line in the early evening after the passenger services had ended for the day and being unloaded from a special siding which had been laid in for the purpose. Similar, smaller-scale, work has been carried out since. On the passenger side excursion trains from various parts of the main-line network have been working in regularly since the 1990s.

The water tower at Minehead MPD. *Peter Townsend*

Today the West Somerset Railway is one of the largest visitor attractions in South West England, carrying some 200,000 passengers per annum. It employs around 50 people and has a volunteer work force of 1000 or so. The volunteers come from far and wide with some working several days a week (sometimes in two or three different roles) and others only able to do a dozen or so turns a year. All staff are trained to the national standards appropriate to the jobs they are carrying out.

A journey along the line

Before the description starts it's necessary to look at the descriptive terminology used and the references to "up" and "down" sides of the train. This does not mean that the WSR uses tilting trains or that they have a permanent list to one side!

"Up" trains on the Great Western Railway and most other British railways meant that they were heading towards London whilst "down" trains were proceeding away from the English capital. So as the train makes its way from Bishops Lydeard to Minehead the up side is on the right and the down side on the left. The opposite applies if you are travelling from Minehead to Bishops Lydeard.

2-6-2T No 4561 skirts the coast as it travels towards Bishops Lydeard. *Alan Turner*

The Norton Fitzwarren line

Passengers coming to the WSR from the motorway or national rail network normally start their journey at Bishops Lydeard station and make their journeys towards Minehead. However, there is a section of line between Bishops Lydeard and Norton Fitzwarren Junction which is used by excursion trains from the main line and during gala and other special events. When the main line is left the main feature is on the down side in the form of the large turning triangle constructed to allow locomotives to change the way they face by running round it. During the early 2010s the area was also used for offloading spent ballast from track renewals on the West of England main line, the High Output Ballast Cleaning Train being worked on and off the WSR by Freightliner Heavy Haul diesel locomotives. The triangle incorporates a short section of the old route of the Taunton to Barnstaple branch line, closed in 1966, but there is no intention by the West Somerset to open any more. Norton Fitzwarren platform exists to serve the "Rally Fields" exhibition site which is where the Steam Fayre and Vintage Rally is held annually at the start of August. The platform does not see regular services and there is no public access to it by car or on foot. On the up side the trains pass the Norton Manor Camp, home of 40 Commando Royal Marines, then sidings and the loco servicing facility before they reach Bishops Lydeard station.

BISHOPS LYDEARD

Standing on the edge of the village and adjacent to the Broad Gauge Industrial Park, Bishops Lydeard has seen many changes during the "preservation era". Between 1862 and 1971 it was a quiet wayside station but has had to be adapted to cope with its role as the southern terminus of the WSR.

Today most trains arrive at and depart from the one-time up platform and this has been lengthened so that the signal box now stands in the platform rather than at the Taunton end of it. The extension also created a third platform face and this bay platform was planned to be able to accommodate four-car diesel multiple unit trains when there was an intention by the Regional Railways sector of British Rail to run seasonal trains from Gloucester and Cardiff to Bishops Lydeard in the 1990s. This got "lost" during rail privatisation and the bay is now normally used to house the "Quantock Belle" dining car set.

The signal box and the wooden waiting room on the up platform date from pre-preservation but the large wooden building which houses the booking office and café/shop has been specially built. The booking office is now in its third location having been previously sited in the original station building, and then at the foot of the ramp from the car park to the platform. Over on the down platform the original station building now serves as an office and staff mess room whilst the goods shed houses the "Gauge Museum", open on days when trains are

Station notes

Opened: 1862
Closed: 1971
Reopened: 1979
Ownership:
West Somerset Railway
Great Western Railway
British Railways
West Somerset Railway
Platforms: Two
Signal box: Yes
Toilets: Yes (RADAR)
Café: Yes
Shop: Yes
Platform access:
Easy access – shallow ramp to platform

Through trains from the main-line network appear regularly on the West Somerset, and here we see 'A1' Class 'Pacific' No 60163 *Tornado* drawing the crowds at Bishops Lydeard as it heads towards Minehead. *Brian Pibworth*

The climate of Taunton Deane and West Somerset is very mild, and pictures of trains in frost and snow are not easy to obtain. Here GWR 'Small Prairie' is running round its train at Bishops Lydeard in the post-Christmas services period. *Claire Rickson*

running. The upstairs area of the Museum houses a large 4 mm scale model railway. Between the station building and the Museum is the club room of the Taunton Model Railway Group which is open to the public on selected dates through the year, usually during Galas and other enthusiast-targeted events. The layouts of the TMRG have won awards and are fine examples of the modeller's arts.

Looking ito the future there are major plans afoot for the further development of Bishops Lydeard. During the life of this edition of the Guide the locomotives standing in the compound should acquire a roof over them and a large water tank acquired from the former locomotive depot at Reading is due to be erected to replace a former industrial example from Ilminster which came to Bishops Lydeard in 1991. Other plans include more siding and storage shed space.

Bishops Lydeard to Crowcombe Heathfield

The train leaves Bishops Lydeard station and passes under the bridge carrying the road to Halse and Ash Priors and then between the Greenway Estate on the down side and the grounds of the Royal British Legion Residential Care Home, Dunkirk House, on the up. At this point the line becomes single and the climb into the Quantock Hills begins as the train goes into

A Crowcombe Heathfield station volunteer watches British Railways (Western Region) No 7828 *Odney Manor* arriving at the station with a train for Minehead. *Ian Smith*

a cutting. Emerging from this you pass over a foot crossing called "Whiskey Trail" after its use by United States airmen in the Second World War making their way to the pubs in Bishops Lydeard village. As the line runs on an embankment and crosses the bridge over the Monksilver road the village can be seen on the up side with Cedar Falls Health Farm in the foreground. From here on the views from the windows are of the "each a glimpse" type and the railway line twice crosses the A358 road as the train passes through the hamlet of Combe Florey. The large house on the hill on the down side was formerly the family home of the novelist Evelyn Waugh and his journalist son Auberon. Evelyn mentions a "Combe Florey Halt" in one of his novels but in fact there has never been any station here. The train now goes off into the hills and leaves the roads behind, continuing its climb through the Area of Outstanding Natural Beauty that is the Quantock Hills until the top of the incline is reached and the train runs under a high bridge and arrives at Crowcombe Heathfield station.

CROWCOMBE HEATHFIELD

It was in the 1960s that Crowcombe Heathfield station had its widest worldwide exposure when the Beatles were filmed riding bicycles on the down -side platform as part of their first feature film "A Hard Day's Night". Apart from the sequence of the "Fab Four" running into the station at the start (that was London Marylebone) the on-train sequences were filmed aboard a special train on the Minehead line. Schools in Minehead followed a realistic path and gave pupils time off when this was going on. The remote location has made it popular with production units and it has also appeared in "The Land Girls" and TV series such as "The Flockton Flier".

The station was one of those which were severely affected by the cut-backs during the last years of the British Rail era and since reopening much work has gone into making good what was lost. So the passing loop line has been reinstated and signalling installed. The present signal box has a new brick base but the wooden top came from South Wales. The station building has been extended to accommodate a toilet facility for disabled passengers and there are other improvements being made by the Friends of Crowcombe Heathfield Station as fund-raising allows. At the Minehead

Station notes

Opened: 1862
Closed: 1971
Reopened: 1979
Ownership:
West Somerset Railway
Great Western Railway
British Railways
West Somerset Railway
Platforms: Two
Signal box: Yes
Toilets: Yes
Café: Yes
Shop No
Platform access:
Grassed area level to platform

Cycles are carried in the guards vans of the 1950s coaching stock of the railway. Here a large group of cyclists who have enjoyed the quiet roads in the Quantock Hills await a train at Crowcombe Heathfield. *Tim Stanger*

In the first of these views of contrasting trains and weather at Crowcombe Heathfield, S&DJR No 88 double-heads with GWR 'Small Prairie' No 5553 on the approach to Crowcombe Heathfield. The signalman braves the bitter cold to exchange the single-line token.

In the second image 'The Quantock Belle' arrives behind No 4160. The signalman again exchanges the token. *WSR collection/Tim Stanger*

end of the down platform there is a short length of Brunel's original broad gauge track for those who would like to see how this looked on the line until 1882. The station is a popular start and finish point for walkers and its home-made refreshments are always welcomed by passengers.

The snow-covered winter scene is picturesque, but does not seem to have brought many visitors. *WSR Collection*

On a bright sunny day 'Hymek' No D7017 stands at Crowcombe Heathfield awaiting a service due from Bishops Lydeard to clear the section. This will release the token to enable No D7017 to enter the single line towards Bishops Lydeard. *Kelvin Lumb*

Crowcombe Heathfield to Stogumber

Having passed the highest point on the line just before reaching Crowcombe Heathfield station the line now starts the descent through the Quantocks towards the coast. As the train pulls away from Crowcombe

An evocative view of the West Somerset Railway in the Quantock Hills as GWR 'Small Prairie' No 5542 heads a train near Cotford Bridge. *Sam Burton*

Above: Great Western Railway-designed 'Mogul' No 9351 completes the long climb from Williton and arrives at Crowcombe Heathfield station with a train for Minehead. The former Station Master's house 'Puff Cottage' is in the background. *Keith Smith*

Heathfield station it passes a raised bank on the up side which was once the trackbed for a siding used in loading stone from the local quarries, while on the up side the former station master's house can be seen. It is now a private home. The train passes a number of crossings with minor roads and then over a road bridge before entering Stogumber station

Right: Not a daily scene on the WSR, but here we see a London & South Western Railway Beattie well tank engine dating from the 1870s trundling a short demonstration freight train through the Quantocks. The locomotive was hired from the Bodmin & Wenford Railway for a steam gala event. *Martin Southwood*

STOGUMBER

This page and opposite top: The unusual layout of Stogumber station is captured here with the chimney of the station building on the right and the platform on the left as No 6960 *Raveningham Hall* waits with a train for Bishops Lydeard. In the picture opposite a diesel multiple unit is rather overshadowed by the splendid garden and picnic area. Does a cream tea at this location look tempting? They are served in the summer between May and October. *Sylvia Way/Alan Turner*

This small wayside station is cut out of the hillside and as a result the layout is very unusual. Looking out on the up side you will see the station building at ground level whilst the platform is on the down.As with Crowcombe Heathfield the station is popular with walkers and on fine days also attracts passengers and visitors who like to sit in the gardens where the goods yard and shed once were and enjoy picnics or the station's home-made refreshments. The station's Friends group has plans to restore the former cattle dock and a cattle wagon to recreate the days when livestock was carried by rail. A country walk is needed to reach Stogumber village from the station. Leaving

Station notes

Opened: 1862
Closed: 1971
Reopened: 1978
Ownership:
West Somerset Railway
Great Western Railway
British Railways
West Somerset Railway
Platforms: One
Signal box: No
Toilets: Yes
Café: Yes
Shop: No
Platform access:
Too narrow – steep ramp to platform

Station Fact

For many years the late Harry Horne had a good claim to the title of 'world's oldest station master', greeting passengers at Stogumber until his death in his tenth decade. After his passing his widow Iris continued as station master until just before her own death. Harry features in the book *Tales of the Old Railwaymen*.

the station by the main building turn right under the railway bridge and carry on past the one-time "Railway Hotel" on the right. The road undulates up and down en route to the village which has a pub, church and local shop. If you visit the pub, "The White Horse", you'll see a poster on the wall from the former Stogumber Brewery which closed in the 1930s. Stogumber village has hosted regular music festivals in late summer in recent years, mainly featuring classical and folk performers.

Stogumber to Williton

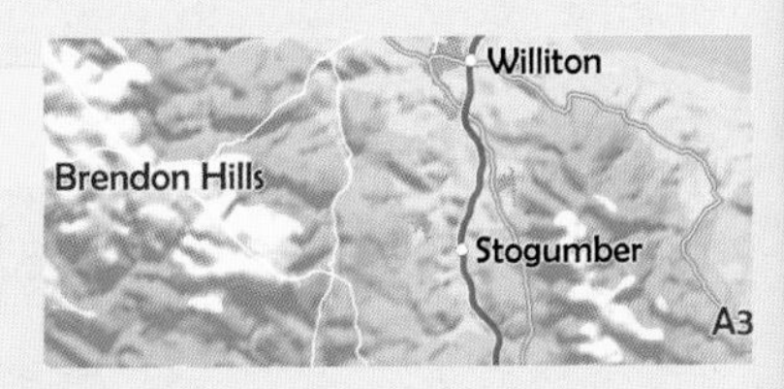

Leaving Stogumber the train continues on its descent, heading out of the Quantocks and with views of the Brendon Hills and Exmoor beginning to open out on the down side and the Quantocks heading to meet the Bristol Channel some distance from the line at West Quantoxhead on the up. The main A358 road reappears on the up side as the train crosses Woolston Moor and then after passing the hamlet of Sampford Brett on the down side goes under the line before the train runs along a shelf cut at the foot of Castle Hill with a small river on the down side. Emerging from a cutting the large village of Williton can be viewed on the down side and then the train reaches Williton station.

British Railways Western Region No 7828 *Odney Manor* leaves Williton and approaches Castle Hill with a train for Bishops Lydeard. *Alan Turner*

WILLITON

Williton station stands on the edge of the large village and if you are going into the centre allow 15 minutes for the walk. In the centre you will find a bank, a number of local shops, pubs and an Indian restaurant. If you are heading for the Bakelite Museum it is sensible to allow 30-35 minutes walking time as this is right at the other end of the village.

Train movements at the station are controlled by the signal box at the Bishops Lydeard end of the down platform. Dating from 1862 this is the only working example of a Bristol and Exeter Railway box still in use. The down platform also has the original station building which houses the

Station notes

Opened: 1862
Closed: 1971
Reopened: 1976
Ownership:
West Somerset Railway
Great Western Railway
British Railways
West Somerset Railway
Platforms: Two
Signal box: Yes
Toilets: No
Café: Yes
Shop: No
Platform access:
Narrow – shallow ramp to platform

Top: British Railways (Western Region) No 7828 *Odney Manor* leaves Williton station and prepares for the long climb to the summit of the West Somerset Railway at Crowcombe Heathfield. The Bristol and Exeter Railway signal box is on the left of the picture. *Audrey Mills*

Above: Williton is the archetypal passing station. As the mid-point of the railway things become busy when two trains are passing here but after these have departed quiet often descends. The former Trowbridge station footbridge is adjacent to the former up platform waiting room which is now the fund-raising shop for the station. *Edward Shepperd*

booking office and there is a café between the signal box and the building. The up side platform has a small wooden waiting room which is used as a fund-raising shop for the station. For passengers wishing to cross over the running lines there is a footbridge which formerly stood at Trowbridge and was brought to the station and erected to replace one removed by British Rail.

On the down side the sidings house a number of vintage diesel locomotives. These are part of the fleet maintained by the Diesel and Electric Preservation Group, volunteers who are dedicated to keeping these machines dating from the 1950s and 60s in working order. Starting out in the Williton goods shed they have subsequently built a depot building and a Heritage Centre which is open on Saturdays and on Gala days. Admission is by donation. Beyond this on the down side is a large corrugated iron building. Once part of the Great Western workshops at Swindon, where it was known as the "Crystal Palace", it was donated to the WSR and is now used by West Somerset Restorations and the West Somerset Steam Railway Trust working on historic locomotives and vehicles. This area is not generally open to the public but often welcomes them on Saturdays and Sundays during Gala events.

Above: 'King Arthur' Class No 30777 *Sir Lamiel* makes a spectacular departure from Williton with an up train towards Bishops Lydeard. The locomotive spent the spring of 2011 on hire to the West Somerset Railway and is the only surviving example of this class of express locomotives built for the Southern Railway. *WSR Collection*

Below: West Somerset Restorations has a thriving apprenticeship scheme and apprentice Ryan Pope has worked to return a Barclay industrial shunting locomotive to full working order. It was completed in 2016 and shows how traditional engineering skills are being maintained and carried forward for the future. *Duncan Hensley*

Williton to Watchet via Doniford Halt

On leaving Williton the line curves away towards the coast and passes through Doniford Halt. The Halt was built by the WSR in the 1980s with a view to picking up traffic from the Haven Holiday Centre and utilises the platform from Montacute station on the one-time Taunton-Yeovil branch line (closed in 1964) and a Great Western Railway "pagoda" shelter which originated at Cove on the Exe Valley line whose trains linked Exeter St Davids and Dulverton (closed 1963). In more recent times a popular family farm attraction has opened and it is hoped to build a path between it and the Halt to make access easier than the walk along the main road which has no pavement. After Doniford Halt the trains run along the cliff tops and it is salutary to realise than when the line opened in 1862 this section was comfortably inland. Looking across the Bristol Channel the area of South Wales visible on the up side is that around Cardiff and Penarth. Also visible are the two islands in the Channel, Flatholme and Steepholme. Neither of these is now inhabited and are bird sanctuaries.

A visiting 'Black 5' locomotive heads a train towards Bishops Lydeard along the cliff-top section at Doniford. When the line was originally built it was nearly 100 yards inland at this point, reflecting the problems of protecting the line for the future against coastal erosion and the tide range of the Bristol Channel. *Sam Burton*

DONIFORD HALT

Halt notes

Opened: 1987
Ownership:
West Somerset Railway
Platforms: One
Signal box: No
Toilets: No
Café: No
Shop: No
Platform access:
Very difficult – small uneven gravel path leads down from road embankment with gated entrance (and no car parking).

Above right: The intending passenger's view of Doniford Halt as seen from the approach path, providing a good view of the Great Western Railway 'pagoda' shelter and the platform looking towards Williton. *WSR Collection*

Below: The old-time charm of the Great Western branch lines is evoked by a GWR steam railcar arriving at Doniford Halt during a Steam Gala event. The railcar was hired from the Didcot Railway Centre, home of the Great Western Railway Society, where it can normally be seen and travelled on. *Stephen Edge*

The Halt dates from the mid-1980s, with the platform on the up side, and was built primarily to serve the Haven Holiday Centre at Doniford Bay. In more recent years a popular family farm attraction has been established close to the Halt. Although of more recent construction than the other stations on the line it incorporates the platform from Montacute (on the Taunton-Yeovil line closed in 1964) and the GWR "pagoda" shelter from Cove (on the Exe Valley line closed in 1963). Please note: If you are walking to or from the Halt there is no pavement and the road is narrow with some sharp bends.

Doniford Halt to Watchet

After leaving the Halt trains run out on to a cliff-top section with good views across the Bristol Channel and in the distance along the coast the nuclear power station at Hinckley Point on the up side. On the down side the houses on the edge of Watchet begin to appear. This section of the route is closely monitored as there has been considerable coastal erosion since the line was first built. The train continues on its journey through a cutting past the Watchet Sports Ground (at least one carriage has been hit by a mighty blow for six during the cricket season) and enters the terminus of the original West Somerset Railway.

Below: A lovely sunny day as Great Western Railway-designed No 9351 leaves Doniford Halt with a train heading towards Watchet and running on to the cliff-top section of the line above Doniford Bay.*John Ewart*

Above: An unusual visitor to the WSR and Watchet station. USA 6046 (an American design of heavy freight locomotive dating from World War 2) departs for Minehead during a Steam Gala event. *Kelvin Lumb*

WATCHET

The most obvious sign that Watchet station was built as a terminus is the layout of the station itself with its main building at right-angles to the running line. On the platform there is another "pagoda" building which houses a photographic display of scenes from the railway's past and a stone building used as a store. The interior of the main building has been adapted by the station's support group and now has a sales stand, light refreshments and a room given over to the sale of second-hand books with the proceeds helping to fund the station maintenance and improvements. The former goods shed is now no longer owned by the railway but houses the Watchet Boat Museum, open on afternoons in the main holiday season between 14.00 and 16.00. The former network of lines which served the dock has all been lifted and the very tall signal box that controlled them from the station platform has long since been demolished (as it would overlook neighbouring properties and there is only a single line of track through the station now there is no intention to reinstate it).

Above: The long platform at Watchet station curves towards Bishops Lydeard, the Goviers Lane exit from the station on to the Quay, and the old harbour, which is now a Marina. *Sam Burton*

Below: This picture demonstrates how the station building at Watchet was originally built as a terminus, standing at right-angles to the track and with the embankment at the rear cut away to make room for it. *Sam Burton*

Station notes

Opened:	1862
Closed:	1971
Reopened:	1976
Ownership:	
West Somerset Railway	
Great Western Railway	
British Railways	
West Somerset Railway	
Platforms:	Two
Signal box:	No
Toilets:	Yes
Café:	No
Shop:	Yes
Platform access:	
Easy – level access to platform	

The station stands in the heart of the town and it's a short walk past the marina, which now gives a new role to the old commercial harbour, to the Town Museum which tells much of Watchet's 1,000 years of history including the shipping and the West Somerset Mineral Railway. There are statues on the quay side. One represents the Ancient Mariner, the doomed principal in the

Above: This nocturnal picture again shows Watchet's station building standing at right-angles to the running line, reflecting the station's original status as a terminus between 1862 and 1874. *Keith Smith*

Below: No 7828 (originally *Odney Manor* but temporarily renamed *Norton Manor 40 Commando*) arrives with a down train during the 2011 Autumn Steam Gala. *Julian Moore*

Watchet harbour

The last commercial traffic used the port of Watchet in the 1990s, since when the harbour has become a marina and a source of business for the regeneration of the town as a whole. Trains once ran on to the quays for loading; one of the last commercial cargoes to be carried was esparto grass from Spain, which was used in the local Watchet Paper Mill and also taken by rail to the mill at Hele and Bradninch on the main line between Taunton and Exeter.

epic poem by Samuel Taylor Coleridge who lived in the area for a number of years (his one-time cottage, near Nether Stowey, is now in the care of the National Trust) and the other "Yankee Jack". "Yankee Jack" was local sailor John Short who was born in 1839 and died in 1933. He first went to sea in the local shipping trade at the age of 14 and by the age of 18 was a deep-sea sailor. Having a strong singing voice he became a singer of sea shanties and in 1914 Cecil Sharp, the collector of folk songs, came visiting. The 33 shanties that John Short was able to perform were the basis of one of Sharp's books. Watchet has narrow streets, local shops and a good selection of places to eat and drink. During the summer months there are regular special events held.

Watchet to Washford

On leaving Watchet the train passes under a roadbridge and through a cutting before travelling along a section of embankment with modern housing

Above: No 7820 *Dinmore Manor* leaves Watchet tender first; this is not the most popular way of running for some photographers, but did occur in the days of steam and adds variety. *WSR Collection*

Right: A visitor to the WSR in earlier days, and now awaiting overhaul at Buckfastleigh on the South Devon Railway, Great Western Railway 4-6-0 No 4920 *Dumbleton Hall* leaves Watchet en route to Washford. *WSR Collection*

on the up side and the paper mill appearing on the down. On the hill above the former site of the paper mill the tower of St Decuman's church can be seen, sharing with its site a holy well which usually indicates a pre-Christian religious use. Decuman was a Celtic saint who like many of the number was supposed to have sailed across the Bristol Channel by unlikely means of transport (his cloak) in company of a cow. In the sixth and seventh centuries Celtic saints on stone rafts, altars, etc, must have been a considerable hazard to shipping It is on this short section that the WSR passes over a bridge above the trackbed of the West Somerset Mineral Railway which is in use as a footpath running between the West Somerset and the Washford river until it reaches Washford's playing fields. Leaving Watchet behind the line now starts a continuous climb to Washford with the Mineral Line footpath on the down side and rolling farmland on the up. As the train approaches Washford the old Mineral Line swings away on a low embankment behind the playing fields on the down side. The WSMR had a station at Washford but it was demolished in the 1930s and the site is now private land. Housing is on the up side and the train passes behind the Washford Inn on the down side as it enters the station.

Above: Great Western Railway No 6960 *Raveningham Hall* climbs up Kentsford Bank between Watchet and Washford with the tower of St Decuman's Chuch in the background. *Don Bishop*

Below: British Railways (Western Region) No 7828 *Odney Manor* climbing Kentsford Bank towards Minehead on a beautiful sunny day with a train for Minehead *Alan Turner*

WASHFORD

The weather is brightening as Great Western Railway 'Modified Hall' No 6960 *Raveningham Hall* completes the climb from Blue Anchor and arrives at Washford with a train for Bishops Lydeard. The Somerset and Dorset Railway Trust's Peckett saddle tank *Kilmersdon* shunts in the yard. *Bev Zehetmeier*

Washford station was the first on the Minehead Railway, as distinct from the original West Somerset, and the main station building shows a complete change in architectural style. Today this is further accented by the paint scheme being Southern Region green as distinct from the Great Western styles favoured at the other stations. The reason for this is that since 1976 Washford has been home to the Somerset and Dorset Railway Trust which keeps alive the memories of the route of lines which once linked Bath (Green Park) and Bournemouth West, Evercreech Junction and Burnham-on-Sea, Glastonbury and Wells, and Edington Junction and Bridgwater North.

When the Trust arrived all that was left at the site was the main building and the small signal box with the running line. The present-day buildings and sidings, plus the collection of stock which is either on display or being restored, is the property of the SDRT whilst the station building is now a museum dedicated to the one-time S&D with other exhibits housed in vans around the site. The narrow gauge railway exhibit came from the one time peat works system around Ashcott on the Somerset Levels which crossed the Evercreech-Burnham line.

Washford station is the alighting point for Cleeve Abbey and Torre Cider Farm. The

Station notes

Opened: 1874
Closed: 1971
Reopened: 1976
Ownership:
Minehead Railway
Great Western Railway
British Railways
West Somerset Railway
Platforms: One
Signal box: Yes
Toilets: No
Café: No
Shop: No
Platform access:
Easy – level access to platform

DISABLED PARKING

The Somerset & Dorset Railway Trust

The SDRT came to the West Somerset following the collapse of the Radstock Project, an attempt to bring trains back to part of the old Somerset & Dorset line. Having moved in at Washford, the Trust laid track, put up buildings and established a restoration base and museum dedicated to the much-missed S&D. The Trust's largest single possession is 7F 2-8-0 No 88, which has been working trains on the West Somerset since 1987. Opening times depend on the availability of volunteers, but the contact phone number is 01984 640869.

Above: The SDRT's 7F 2-8-0 No 88 is seen awaiting departure from Crowcombe Heathfield.

main road through the village is narrow and has high stone walls and the signposted safe walking route to the Abbey is the one to follow. Cleeve was a Cistercian establishment and a major land owner until the dissolution in the 16th Century. After this the main church was demolished and used by local residents as a source of building stone but the out buildings have survived and give visitors a great insight into monastic life. The Abbey is now in the care of English Heritage and opens between Easter and October.

Above: 2-6-2T No 4160 has a good head of steam on departure from Washford heading towards Blue Anchor. The primroses are out and bring a touch of nature to the neatly trimmed cutting and tree line. *WSR Collection*

Continuing along the road past the Abbey take the left-hand fork at the road junction at the "White Horse" and bear round to the left over the site of a level crossing on the erstwhile Mineral Line to reach the Cider Farm. Somerset cider is a very fine drink but treat it with respect. The local dialect term for a cider hangover was being "hammered" which is all that needs to be said on the subject. Walking time from the station to the Abbey is around 20 minutes and add on another 10 to Torre Farm.

Washford to Blue Anchor

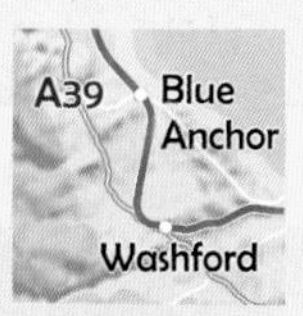

From Washford the train descends through a cutting on what is the most steeply graded section of the line (1 in 65). Emerging from the cutting the village of Bilbrook can be seen on the down side with the Brendon Hills and Exmoor as a backdrop and Old Cleeve on the up as the train continues along an embankment passing over the "Monks' Path" on the way. Prone to flooding, this particular path can easily be mistaken for a stream after a few days of rain. The train leaves the embankment, with static caravans and mobile homes appearing ahead on the up side, onto the coastal plain and swings left through a shallow cutting into Blue Anchor station.

Great Western Railway designed-'Mogul' No 9351 rounds the curve as a train for Bishops Lydeard nears the top of the 1 in 65 climb from Blue Anchor to Washford, the steepest section of the WSR. *Alan Turner*

BLUE ANCHOR

Station notes

Opened: 1904
Closed: 1971
Reopened: 1976
Ownership:
Great Western Railway
British Railways
West Somerset Railway
Platforms: Two
Signal box: Yes
Toilets: No
Café: No
Shop: No
Platform access:
Narrow – shallow ramps

Historically the story of Blue Anchor station is surprisingly complicated for a wayside station adjacent to a Bristol Channel beach. It was opened seemingly as a speculative venture in the hope that holiday traffic would bring a settlement for it to serve and originally had a single platform on the up side, closest to beach and sea. This seems to have used existing buildings to provide passenger facilities and there is no resemblance between these and other Minehead Railway structures. There is a rumour that for a period the station was known as Bradley Gate and the origin of the name Blue Anchor is not precisely known. One story is that it was the colour of mud on anchors when ships moored in the bay, but how much blue mud have you seen? There are some days

It does sometimes snow on the Bristol Channel coast. Great Western 'Large Prairie' No 4160 runs around its train during a 'Santa Special' duty in December 2010. *Sam Burton*

when the angle of the sun produces a distinctive blue lighting effect on the surface of the sea.

Developments at the station saw the passing loop installed and the signal box which is a standard Great Western Railway design, dating in this case from 1904. The signalman also controls the level crossing gates by traditional means of a large wheel at one end of the 'box. The seafront road swings sharply round behind the signal box and directly onto the crossing so the signalman has to be particularly aware of traffic on the road as well as train movements. The small brick building on the down platform now houses a small museum of relics of the Great Western Railway and the Western Region of British Railways and is part of the work of the West Somerset Steam Railway Trust. It is usually open on Sundays, Bank Holidays and during Gala events. Both the signal box and the museum have appeared in 4mm scale model form courtesy of Bachmann Ltd and during December the main up side station building becomes a grotto during "Santa Special" operations when the traditional fires in the grates are welcome.

If you are leaving the train here it's worth stopping for a while to look ahead at the view around the curve of Blue Anchor Bay. In the middle distance is Dunster Castle and the hilltop Conygar Tower and beyond that the distinctive skyline of Butlin's Minehead

Above left: Token exchange between fireman and signalman as an up train arrives from Minehead. *Ian Smith*

Above right: A panoramic view around the sweep of the coastal section between Blue Anchor and Dunster. The village of Dunster is behind the smoke of 'Mogul' No 9351 as it approaches Blue Anchor station with a train from Minehead. The Conygar Tower folly can be seen on the hill. *Alan Turner*

Above left: GWR heavy freight tank engine No 4247 makes a guest appearance during a Gala and hauls a ballast train over the level crossing and into the station. *Keith Smith*

and North Hill, where Exmoor meets the Bristol Channel. When leaving the station be careful. The exit is via a wicket gate beside the signal box and puts you directly onto the bend in the road. A right turn takes you along the seafront which is largely given over to mobile home holiday sites. The Driftwood Café isclose to the station whilst further along is the "Smugglers" pub. Right at the far end of the front is the "Blue Anchor Hotel" which is recent times has lost a large section of its garden to coastal erosion.

Blue Anchor to Dunster

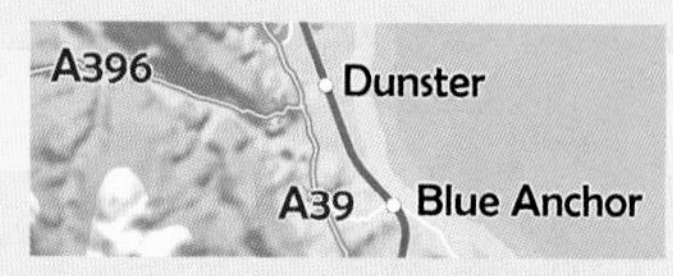

For the rest of its journey the train is running along the coastal plain with views to South Wales, and between Blue Anchor and Dunster it runs on the inland of two shingle ridges which offer flood protection against the Bristol Channel at times of high tides and/or onshore gales. The Bristol Channel has the second highest tidal range in the world and this can be appreciated by passengers who travel by the first trains in the morning and the last in the afternoon as the view on the seaward side of the train can change considerably in that time. Midway along this part of the journey the train passes over the flood relief channel of the River Avill whose purpose is obvious in wetter periods of the year but can be a talking point when it is dry and the wide and shallow trough causes plenty of speculation. Dunster Castle becomes visible on the landward side (it can be surprisingly hard to spot it against the backdrop of the hills in some lighting conditions) and the train passes over an ungated level crossing as it enters Dunster station.

2-6-2T No 4160 (not presently on the WSR) makes an impressive site with a five-coach train heading towards Minehead and the seaside! *WSR Collection*

DUNSTER

Station notes

Opened: 1874
Closed: 1971
Reopened: 1976
Ownership:
Minehead Railway
Great Western Railway
British Railways
West Somerset Railway
Platforms: One
Signal box: Yes
Toilets: No
Café: No
Shop: No
Platform access:
Easy – level access to platform

After the unusual collection of structures at Blue Anchor Dunster station returns to Minehead Railway architectural style. If it seems familiar to railway modellers this is because it was the prototype for the "Country Station" building in the Hornby range for a number of years. The interior houses a small sales area and the ticket office whilst in a back room there is a printing press which produces the traditional style Edmondson card railway tickets for both the West Somerset and other heritage railways. Until the railway came this area was known as "Rotten Row" and was adjacent to the former harbour. Today it is known as the Marsh Street area. The station yard

Left: Rather older than the West Somerset Railway, Dunster Castle has stood above its village for more than 1,000 years and is today in the care of the National Trust. It is a popular destination for WSR passengers who can either take the 20-25-minute walk from the station or arrive via the coach link from the popular 'Dunster Castle Express' trains. *Steve Guscott*

is now home to the WSR's Permanent Way Department which maintains track, fencing, bridges and other structures along the line. According to local tradition the goods shed is haunted by a railwayman killed in a shunting accident. The Minehead end of the platform is cut off short rather than having

Above: British Railways (Western Region) No 7828 *Odney Manor* arrives at a quiet Dunster station with a train for Minehead. The supposedly haunted goods shed is in the background *Ian Grady*

Left: Great Western '64xx' Class pannier tank No 6430 stands at Dunster station with an 'auto-train' passenger working during a Gala. For three decades classmate No 6412 was based on the line before its owner, the West Somerset Railway Association, sold it to the South Devon Railway to part-fund purchase of No 7821 *Ditcheat Manor*. *Sam Burton*

the usual ramp, a reminder of the days when Dunster had a signal box sited at this point and there was double track between here and Minehead.

It is a 20-minute walk from the station to the village, with the final section being steadily up hill, but it rewards those who undertake the journey. The main street is dominated by the 1,000-year-old castle at the far end which is now in the care of the National Trust. Other buildings of historic interest include the Yarn Market, the working water mill and the packhorse bridge. The church has an impressive interior and the "Luttrell Arms" has its origins as a guest house for Cleeve Abbey. There is a Dolls Museum to visit and a wide range of shops and places to eat and drink. On the first Friday and Saturday in December the village hosts the annual "Dunster by Candlelight" evenings when the village goes over to softer lighting and hosts entertainment in the street to go with late-night opening. The WSR runs special trains from Bishops Lydeard as part of the event. It is a short walk to Dunster Beach on the seaward side.

Dunster to Minehead

Great Western Railway-designed 'Mogul' No 9351 crosses the road as it arrives at Dunster station. *Colin Harris*

The train leaves Dunster over another ungated level crossing and travels over coastal marshland towards Minehead. As said earlier this section once had double track but it was singled during the run-down of the line in the 1960s. On the down side the Minehead sewage treatment works can be seen and then the Butlin's Holiday Centre appears on the up. This continues all the way to the point where the train passes over the Seaward Way level crossing and reaches the end of the journey.

MINEHEAD

Right: Flower beds, water tower and Class 25 diesel No 7612 at Minehead. *WSR Collection*

Left: 'A1' 'Pacific' No 60163 *Tornado* is one of the best-known steam locomotives following its construction through the 1990s and early 2000s, and it has visited the West Somerset on a number of occasions, attracting large crowds to see and travel behind it. Here *Tornado* arrives at Minehead as the signalman returns to his box after accepting the single-line token for the section from Blue Anchor. *Sam Burton*

Today Minehead is the headquarters of the West Somerset Railway and as a result has changed greatly from the station as it was in earlier parts of its history. The original station building was expanded in the past as traffic grew in the Great Western era and the long platform, which has two faces for handling trains, is nearly a quarter-mile in length from the entrance gate to the end of the ramp. The latest addition to the station building is the current booking office which dates from the 1980s and incorporates parts of the former booking facility at Cardiff General (now Central) station in its woodwork. Inside the building you will now find a shop and offices plus the toilets.

The one-time locomotive shed was demolished during the 1950s and today the steam locomotive running and repair facility is housed in the former goods shed which has been extended to cope with its changed role. The shed and workshops are not open to the public. Where the loco shed once stood is now a council-owned car park but Minehead has a locomotive turntable once more following the extension in length and reinstallation of the one rescued from Pwllheli in the early days of the revival. Beside the turntable area is the station café and under the canopy between the two platform faces is the "Reader's Halt" stall which sells a variety of second-hand goods, mainly books and magazines, as a fund-raiser for the upkeep and improvement of the station.

Across the car park a small brick building can be

Station notes

Opened: 1874
Closed: 1971
Reopened: 1976
Ownership:
Minehead Railway
Great Western Railway
British Railways
West Somerset Railway
Platforms: Two
Signal box: Yes
Toilets: Yes RADAR
Café: Yes
Shop: Yes
Platform access:
Level and easy access to platforms

DISABLED PARKING

seen. This was once stabling for railway delivery horses but in more recent times has been home to an amateur boxing club.

On leaving the station North Hill is directly ahead with part of the old town visible on its slope. A right turn takes visitors along the sea front towards Butlin's and the golf club whilst if you go straight ahead the promenade ends at the harbour. This is also the route for walkers starting along the South West Coast Path, a route that goes via Land's End to end at Poole in Dorset. By turning left visitors make their way into the town centre with a mixture of national chain shops and local businesses. As you would expect in a seaside resort town there is a wide choice of eating and drinking establishments.

Above: With North Hill forming a backdrop, No 7828 *Norton Manor 40 Commando* (renamed from *Odney Manor* to mark the WSR's close relations with its neighbours at Norton Manor Camp) shunts into Platform 2 at Minehead station. The footplate crew are obviously enjoying a verbal exchange with the signalman. *Sam Burton*

Below: The WSR has held a number of gala events based on the anniversaries of closure of the much-missed Somerset & Dorset line, which closed in March 1966. During the 2006 Spring Gala a typical S&D express working was recreated with the arrival at Minehead of BR Standard 4MT 'Mogul' No 76009 and Bulleid 'Battle of Britain' 'Pacific' No 34067 *Tangmere*, bringing back memories of a time when this combination of loco classes would appear at Bournemouth West. *Claire Rickson*

MINEHEAD
What to see and do nearby

Today's passenger arriving at Minehead has a choice of directions and destinations to follow from the station entrance. A left turn across the adjacent car park brings you to the Minehead Eye; this exciting and innovative project provides a dedicated, purpose-built extreme sports skate park and youth centre.

A right turn takes you along the seafront towards Butlins Resort. The path continues past the centre and the golf course and can be followed to Dunster Beach and Blue Anchor.

Passengers looking for the beach have simply to cross the road, and there it is.

Crossing the road and walking along the esplanade takes you towards the tall feature of North Hill. Along the way you pass the start of the South West Coast Path, which if followed in its entirety will take you to Poole Harbour via Land's End in Cornwall. The road eventually reaches the harbour, where historic ships the *Waverley* and the *Balmoral* pay their periodic visits to the town, bringing loads of visitors (and some passengers to the railway) in an evocation of the great days of Bristol Channel shipping. For those seeking some quiet and tranquillity, turning off the esplanade and up into North Hill is recommended, but be aware that there is some hard hill-climbing involved.

The left turn out of the station takes you past the Beach Hotel, popular with coach companies as a base for touring the area, and into the main shopping area of the town. Here there is the usual mixture of seaside souvenir shops and the more specialised outlets, the latter being further from the seafront.

As you would expect, there is a variety of accommodation to suit all pockets in Minehead, and apart from the railway journey it is a good base to explore Exmoor and the Quantock Hills.

Above: A view of Minehead from the peace and quiet of the Old Town on North Hill, away from the bustle of the seaside town below it. The Butlins Pavilion dominates the distant view while the more venerable tower of St Michael's Church is closer to the photographer. *Sam Burton*

Left: The busy platform at Minehead is seen from the footplate of a GWR pannier tank locomotive. *Sam Burton*

The Steam Locomotive Fleet – *a selection...*

Loco No	Class	Wheel Arr	Designer/Builder	Year built	Weight
Ex-Great Western Railway					
4936 *Kinlet Hall*	4900 5MT	4-6-0	Collett, Swindon	1929	61 tons
4561	4500 4MT	2-6-2T	Churchward, Swindon	1924	57 tons
6960 *Raveningham Hall*	6959 5MT	4-6-0	Hawksworth, Swindon	1944	75 tons 16 cwt
West Somerset Railway					
9351	Mogul	2-6-0	Collett, Minehead	2000-4	
Ex- Southern Railway					
Ex- London Midland & Scottish Railway					
44422	4F	0-6-0	Fowler, Derby		
Ex-London North Eastern Railway					
Ex-Somerset & Dorset Joint Railway					
53808 (S&D No 88)	7F	2-8-0	Fowler, Darlington	1925	64 tons 15 cwt
Ex-British Railways					
7821 *Ditcheat Manor*	7800 5MT	4-6-0	Collett, Swindon	1950	68 tons 18 cwt
7828 *Odney Manor (BR) Norton Manor (WSR)*	7800 5MT	4-6-0	Collett, Swindon	1950	68 tons 18 cwt
Ex-Army					
Ex-Industrial Locos					
Kilmersdon (Saddle Tank)		0-4-0	Peckett, Bristol	1929	

* Please note that the above listing and that of diesels on page 44 are made up of locomotives normally based on the WSR and as at the time of writing. However, throughout the year additional visiting locomotives are often to be seen on the railway. Locomotives from the WSR also visit other locations for galas, events or overhaul.

Some space has been provided to write in visitors and new arrivals.

Top right: Great Western Railway 'Hall' Class No 4936 *Kinlet Hall* at Liddymore, providing good evidence of why the Quantock Hills have been designated an Area of Outstanding Natural Beauty. *Don Bishop*

Middle right: Great Western Railway 'Modified Hall' No 6960 *Raveningham Hall* at the idiosyncratically named Quarkhil Bridge, climbing through the Quantock Hills. *David Smith*

Bottom right: London Midland & Scottish Railway 4F No 44422 heads a demonstration freight train at Nornvis Bridge during a Steam Gala event. *Don Bishop*

Oppsite page: Great Western 'Large Prairie' tank engine No 4110 has been purchased for restoration to working order by the West Somerset Railway. It was built at Swindon in 1936 and in its working career for the Great Western Railway and the Western Region of British Railways it did spend time at Taunton locomotive shed and worked on the line to Minehead. The locomotive has never been in working order since leaving the Barry scrapyard and it has been over half a century since it last worked a train. Hopefully we may see it in action again before the next edition of this guide book is due. *Colin Howard*

Top: Eleven of these heavy freight machines were built for the Somerset & Dorset Joint Railway, the first batch of six in 1914 and the second (which originally had larger-diameter boilers) in 1925. Their main duties were working goods and mineral trains over the steeply graded S&DJR line over the Mendip Hills but at times of peak summer traffic they could also be found on passenger trains whose timings did not require too much by way of high speed. No 53808 is one of two survivors having been purchased from Barry by the Washford-based Somerset and Dorset Railway Trust. It is on hire to the WSR from the Trust. *Peter Townsend*

Middle: Great Western Railway 'Modified Hall' No 6960 *Raveningham Hall.* A 1944 adaptation by F.W. Hawksworth of the original 'Hall' design by C.B. Collett, all of the 'Halls' worked on express trains and fast freight for the GWR and the Western Region of British Railways between 1929 and 1965. *Quentin Hawkes*

Right: LMS 4F No 44422 again, this time on passenger work, curving away from Williton with a passenger train for Minehead. Intended for freight work these locomotives (of which 771 were built) also found themselves on secondary passenger work. *Alan Turner*

Left: Designed by the Great Western Railway in 1936 but not built until the 21st Century when it was constructed at Minehead, No 9351 is a small-boilered 'Mogul' 2-6-0. Intended for use on secondary main line work, the design has proved absolutely ideal for work between Bishops Lydeard and Minehead. It is seen here at Blue Anchor beach. *Steve Edge*

Left: The 'Small Prairies' were designed by G.J. Churchward and for half a century could be found at work on branch lines across the Great Western Railway and the Western Region of British Railways until the mid 1960s. Taunton shed always had an allocation and they worked to Minehead. No 4561 was built at Swindon in 1924 and after being purchased by the West Somerset Railway Association came to the WSR in the 1970s. In 2016 it was being overhauled in the workshops at Williton. *Alan Meade*

Left: Built in 1929 by Peckett in Bristol, *Kilmersdon* was the last steam engine to work in industry in Somerset at the colliery of the same name. Now in the care of the Somerset and Dorset Railway Trust at Washford (hence the splendid, albeit unauthentic livery) it is pictured here in company with Somerset and Dorset Railway carriage number 4 in Washford Yard. *Malcolm Garner*

The Diesel Locomotive Fleet – *a selection...*

Loco No	Class	Wheel Arr	Builder	Year built	Weight
Ex-British Railways					
D1010 *Western Campaigner*	52	C-C	British Railways Swindon Works	1962	108 tons
D7017	35	B-B	Beyer Peacock, Manchester	1962	74 tons
D7018 †	35	B-B	Beyer Peacock, Manchester	1962	74 tons
D9526	14	0-6-0	British Railways Swindon Works	1964	49 tons 6 cwt
D9518 †	14	0-6-0	British Railways Swindon Works	1964	49 tons 6 cwt
D6566	33	Bo-Bo	Bimingham Carriage & Wagon Co	1961	74 tons 4 cwt
D6575 †	33	Bo-Bo	Bimingham Carriage & Wagon Co	1961	74 tons 4 cwt
D1661 *North Star*	47	Co-Co	British Railways Crewe Works	1965	127 tons
D2133	03	0-6-0	British Railways Swindon Works	1960	30 tons 16 cwt
D2271	04	0-6-0	Robert Stephenson & Hawthorn	1958	29 tons 15 cwt
D9019	09	0-6-0	British Railways	1962	49 tons

† denotes locomotive undergoing overhaul or restoration as at February 2012.

Above: BR once had hundreds of small diesel shunting locomotives for lighter shunting work but the disappearance of local freight work saw many withdrawn after short working careers. Class 03 D2133 was built at Swindon in 1960 and was one of four allocated to Taunton where amongst other work they shunted the docks sidings at Bridgwater (now all torn up). After finishing on British Rail the loco became a long-term Bridgwater resident as the shunter at the now closed and demolished British Cellophane works. British Cellophane in turn presented it to the West Somerset and this has produced the historical curiosity that D2133 has never worked outside Somerset. Another of British Railways' small diesel shunters, D2271, was built by Robert Stephenson & Hawthorn in 1958. Together with D2133 it is usually used for shunting duties at Minehead. *Peter Townsend*

Below: Another very successful class of locomotive, the Class 33s were built for the Southern Region by the Birmingham Railway Carriage & Wagon Company in Smethwick, with D6566 and D6575 entering traffic in 1961. Some of the most reliable of the first generation diesels they eventually worked much further afield that their original home in the south of England and have proved popular with crews and enthusiasts. Before leaving main-line service D6566 had become 33048 and D6575 33057. At the time of writing this guide book D6566 is under heavy overhaul at Williton and D6575 is in traffic. *Alan Turner*

Top: Undoubtedly one of the most successful designs of locomotive to run on the railways of Britain, the Class 47s began to emerge from the Brush Engineering Workshops in Loughborough at the start of the 1960s and half a century later some are still at work on the main-lines. No D1661 *North Star* was built at British Railways Crewe workshops and was one of a batch intended for the Western Region which were given names connected with the Great Western Railway (the original *North Star* was the GWR's first successful steam engine). The 47s have worked all forms of traffic in their careers and *North Star* ended its main-line life numbered 47840 as part of the Virgin Trains fleet on Cross Country Trains duty. It is part of the DEPG fleet. *Claire Rickson*

Centre: The 'Hymeks' were a product of Beyer Peacock in Manchester and were another part of the diesel-hydraulic fleet numbering 101 in total. They were viewed as mixed traffic machines to perform the sort of work done in the steam age by the 'Halls' and proved successful in traffic, before standardisation in the early 70s saw their withdrawal. D7017 was the first locomotive to be purchased by the Diesel and Electric Preservation Group who were amongst the first to realise that there was a danger that a large part of British locomotive history could be lost. D7018 soon followed. Both were built in 1962. Their fortunes on the WSR have been mixed. D7017 has been a regular performer on diesel running days but D7018 suffered a major engine failure whilst working an evening dining train and was out of traffic for well over a decade whilst a major overhaul was carried out. *Alan Turner*

Bottom: The 74 members of the 'Western Class' were the most powerful of the various types of diesel hydraulic locomotive which were introduced by the Western Region in the late 1950s and early 1960s and as they were introduced they took over the haulage of the principal express trains on the routes out of Paddington. D1010 was built at Swindon in 1962. The Class 52s proved to be very successful in the work for which they were designed but by the 1970s a desire to standardise the diesel fleet meant the death knell of the WR's hydraulic transmission machines in favour of the more common diesel electric type. 'Campaigner' was originally preserved by Foster Yeoman and stood at the gates of their quarry in the Mendips from which in the early 1970s the 'Westerns' had worked heavy stone trains. In that role the loco was given the identity of a scrapped classmate D1035 *Western Yeoman*. It is now in the care of the Diesel and Electric Preservation Group at Williton. *WSR Collection*

Coaching Stock

The coaches used by the West Somerset Railway are British Railways Mark 1 vehicles. Here we see three of the fleet freshly repainted in British Railways' carmine and cream livery being shunted at Minehead station. *Martin Southwood*

Travellers on the WSR will find themselves seated in British Railways Mark I carriages, a design dating from the 1950s and which continued in production into the middle part of the 1960s. The majority are open plan with bays of four seats arranged around tables but there are a small number with side corridors and compartments (which have become known to many visitors as "Harry Potter coaches".) To meet passenger requirements conversion work has been done to improve travel for passengers unable to leave their wheelchairs and there is one specialised vehicle which can be pre-booked for larger groups of wheelchair users. There is normally a licensed buffet car in service trains.

The "Quantock Belle" set of carriages are also Mark I vehicles used by the West Somerset Railway Association for their dining car trains. For more information about when these trains are operating or private charters please call 01823 433856. The Association also owns a former British Railways inspection saloon vehicle which is available for hire for groups of up to 20 people looking for a special day out. Contact for bookings is as above.

Longer term the West Somerset Steam Railway Trust has the "Heritage Carriages Project" which has the aim of eventually putting into service vintage Great Western vehicles. The first to be restored, as the initial one to be acquired when a bungalow of which it had become part was demolished, is an 1897 sleeping car vehicle. Not suitable for regular use in service trains, it can normally be viewed in the Gauge Museum. Work is advancing steadily on other vehicles at Williton.

The Somerset and Dorset Railway Trust is the owner of four wooden carriage bodies and the first of these was approaching a return to passenger use when these notes were being written at the end of 2015. It will not be a regular part of the daily workings of the West Somerset but may be available to ride in during some special events.

Freight Stock

The West Somerset Railway has a number of vintage freight vehicles in its care which are used for demonstration goods trains during enthusiast galas and also make up the loads for some of the Footplate Experience Courses.

Here 'Mogul' No 9351 trundles a short rake of wagons in open countryside as it starts the climb between Blue Anchor and Washford. *Kelvin Lumb*

Footplate Experience Courses

The West Somerset runs a variety of these courses for people who would like to try their hand at driving steam and diesel locomotives. They are carried out under instruction and supervision by trained staff and give an insight into the workings of the machines and the wider workings of railways.

Above: Footplate Experience Courses are a popular part of the West Somerset's itinerary, and here participants and instructors pose for a photo at the front end of No 9351. *WSR Collection*

Left: 'The office' – hallowed ground for many a schoolboy trainspotter. A visit to the footplate of a steam locomotive was that often elusive dream and to enter was very much by invitation only! It remains 'forbidden territory' for the most part today, but a Footplate Experience Course can make that dream come true! *Peter Townsend*

The Railway Departments

The West Somerset Railway has a paid staff of around 50 but is also reliant on some 1,000 volunteers who help to keep the railway operating and maintained. Both paid and salaried staff work together in all areas of the railway's activities from track maintenance to promotional work. Similarly the most visible members of the workforce, the signalmen, locomotive crews and on-train staff may be paid or enjoying their hobby. All are, however, given appropriate national rail industry training so that regardless of what the volunteer may do in the day job you can be assured that you are in safe hands.

There are many departments involved in the year-round work and these include the following...

Steam locomotive department

Apparently the most glamorous of the jobs this one harks back to the days up to the 1960s when many small boys (and possibly some girls) wanted to be an engine driver when they grew up. There are however other aspects to the job including early starts to get the engine ready for the day and late finishes as ash and other waste has to be disposed of and the locomotive left in a state overnight where it is ready for bringing back to full working state the next day.

Volunteers starting in the locomotive department begin as cleaners, combining the duty of cleaning the engines with learning the basics of how the machines work before starting to go out

Above: Danger – men at work! While awaiting the arrival of another train scheduled to pass theirs at Crowcombe Heathfield, the driver, fireman, trainee fireman and guard take the chance to relax and enjoy their surroundings. *Alan Meade*

Left: : A short break from the exertions of the footplate for the crew of Great Western 'Manor' Class No 7821 *Ditcheat Manor*. *Peter Townsend*

on locomotives and learning the job of the fireman. Once a level of competency has been attained the next grades are Passed Cleaner and, as experience grows, Fireman. Firemen then begin to learn driving skills and become Passed Firemen able to drive if required and finally Driver. However just to keep their hand in some drivers will take a turn on the firing side whilst the fireman has some practical experience in driving. Teamwork is the crucial aspect in keeping the trains moving.

Left: Once the firebox has been raked out, the ash has to be dug out from the pit and taken away for disposal, regardless of rain, frost, wind or blazing sunshine. It is not all glamorous being a driver or a fireman on a steam railway. *Peter Townsend*

Diesel locomotive & DMU department

With the ending of steam on main-line railways in the 1960's and its replacement by diesel traction another generation of enthusiasts grew up with what are now historic machines in their own right. DMUs have been part of the regular operations of the WSR since the start and training is offered to would-be drivers who are already members of the Operating Department (guards and signalmen). A fleet of vintage diesel locomotives is maintained by the Williton-based Diesel and Electric Preservation Group who not only work to keep their 1950s and 60s machines operational but also have a training schedule for drivers and second men.

A full train crew for a diesel multiple unit: driver, ticket inspectors, guard and buffet attendant. *Alan Meade*

Signalling department

There are two distinct aspects to the railway signalling on the railway. The more immediately obvious are the signalmen (the railway uses the traditional term for the job but women are just as welcome as men in this crucial role) in the signal boxes along the line, at Bishops Lydeard, Crowcombe Heathfield, Williton, Blue Anchor and Minehead. They have control over the train movements along the running lines and shunting movements at Bishops Lydeard, Williton and Minehead. Williton and Blue Anchor duties also include control of level crossings where roads cross the running lines. The signalling and points on the line are of historic railway practice controlled by levers in the signal box and with tokens being issued to and received from loco crews to ensure that there is only one train using the single-track sections of the route at one time. The Blue Anchor box also includes a large wheel for control of the level crossing gates.

The equipment worked by the signalmen has of course to be maintained and as semaphore signals and manually worked points disappear from the national network traditional skills are being kept alive. The technicians and general labourers who work in this part of the operation are essential to keeping the trains moving, and it is generally an open-air job.

Above: I see no ships? Signal maintenance can involve the use of binoculars to check for hand signals from colleagues some considerable distance down the line. *Peter Winstanley*

Right: A maintenance engineer carries out remedial work at one of the many lineside boxes. Looking away from Blue Anchor towards Minehead, the Minehead outer distant signal can be seen on the left. *WSR Collection*

Left: The interior of Blue Anchor signal box showing the lever frame, which operates the signals and points, and the large wheel that operates the traditional level crossing gates outside. The cloth on the lever is traditional; by holding it the signalman prevents the well-burnished tops of the levers from becoming tarnished, and maintains the traditionally immaculate working environment. *WSR Collection*

Below: Right away! *Sam Burton*

Guards and Travelling Ticket Inspectors

The Travelling Ticket Inspector's (TTI's) job is one of the keys in keeping the WSR operating into the future by collecting fares and checking tickets. Ticket issuing is by electronic machine, and machines and floats are drawn at the start of the day at each terminal station. It is essential to be able to give passengers correct change and tickets for the day and this may not always be straightforward as a surprising number of people board the train with no clear plan in mind or give surprising answers as to where they wish to go. (Maidenhead instead of Minehead is a regular, and pronouncing Bishops Lydeard is a struggle at times.) TTIs will also be asked questions about the engine heading the train, places of interest to visit and an endless variety of queries that have popped into the heads of passengers.

Starting as a TTI it is possible to move on to train as a Guard and there is considerably more to that job than waving a green flag and blowing a whistle.The Guard is the person in charge of the train and is trained to deal with any problems, small or serious, that arise. Arriving on duty the train has to be checked for faults and prepared and at the end of the day it has to be made fit to stand overnight and to be as ready as possible for its next turn of duty. Guards are also involved in shunting as necessary. Some Passenger Guards also train to work on goods trains, using the heritage freight train wagons, a skilled job involving keeping the train correctly under control on the climbs, descents and curves.

Connecting the vacuum pipes. *Alan Meade*

On-train catering department

This is another role with plenty of interface between the staff and the passengers. The buffet cars on the locomotive-hauled trains are licensed and sell a range of hot drinks, soft drinks, hot and cold snacks, sweets, crisps, etc. The job does include a lot of standing and at the start of the day, and at times during the day, there will be a need to restock the buffet car from stores at Bishops Lydeard or Minehead. Again cash handling is a key part of the job.

Some of the offerings available from the buffet cars on the regular service trains, complete with a tempting bottle of locally brewed ale from Wiveliscombe. *Steve Sagrott*

The Permanent Way department

The permanent way is the track including the ballast, the 100-plus bridges and culverts and 60-plus miles of fencing and gates, all of which need monitoring and maintaining if the railway is going to continue into the future. The company has a full-time maintenance gang but there is also a volunteer team that works in conjunction with them. The materials that are used are heavy but if you are looking for cardiovascular exercise in the open air then this is definitely worth looking at.

Top right: Concentrating hard to empty the correct amount of ballast from a hopper wagon.

Middle: The work of the permanent way maintenance gangs, both paid and volunteer, goes on all year round and all along the line. This is track relaying taking place between Blue Anchor and Dunster.

Below: The rail-mounted digger is put to good use during the relaying work. *All Sam Burton*

Cutting back department

Travelling through an example of the neat cutting back of the foliage on either side of the cutting. 'Castle' Class 4-6-0 No 5051 *Earl Bathurst* approaches Blue Anchor and pays tribute to the famous express 'The Cornishman' which ran from Paddington to Penzance in GWR days and from various locations to Penzance in the British Railways era – including Wolverhampton, Derby, Sheffield and Wakefield. *WSR Collection*

This is not a financial term. With 23 miles of track comes 46 miles of lineside vegetation to control and this is a very lush and fertile part of the world. In addition part of the WSR's appeal to the public is the variety of scenery that can be seen through the carriage windows and passengers expect to view that rather than a continuous green curtain. A lot of the clearance work has to be done on uneven ground and slopes so it helps to be reasonably fit and clear of aches and pains, but it is rewarding to be out in beautiful settings with trains passing close by. You'll also get a healthy weather-influenced appearance.

Badgers move home...

As you would expect in an area like West Somerset and Taunton Deane, lineside plants and animal life thrive. The railway strives to manage its surroundings sensitively, but sometimes unusual problems arise including one in the 1990s when a badger sett began to cause undermining in an embankment. The necessary permissions were obtained and the badgers were relocated to a new home.

Staffing the stations

Fortunately station maintenance and train operation rarely have to take place in conditions like these in a part of the world where snow is rare. This is Crowcombe Heathfield, showing the conditions in which the WSR was able to run a full programme of Christmas trains in December 2010. *Alan Turner*

The 10 stations along the line are supported by their own groups of volunteers who raise money towards their upkeep and improvements. Major structural work is carried out by the company, skilled volunteer teams or professional builders from outside paid for by the funds raised. There are some formally established station "Friends" groups and a chat to the station staff on duty will give you more information if you have a particular favourite. They can also advise you on what roles need fulfilling and what the ongoing projects may be and how you can help. Booking office clerks and sales staff are welcome but so are painters, gardeners and general helpers, particularly cleaners. Minehead station office staff also answer incoming enquiries by telephone and in person and take telephone bookings as well as carrying out other station duties, reflecting the station's role as the headquarters of the railway.

Booking office clerks

All of the stations except Doniford Halt and Washford have booking offices selling traditional Edmondson card railway tickets and some electronic issues. Bishops Lydeard and Minehead are by far the busiest and the ideal is to have two clerks on duty there on operating days. At other stations the level of bookings and the amount of money handled can vary with the time of year. Of course this is a key area for accurate handling of money and record-keeping and clerks may not manage to see too many trains. However, it's a great way to meet the public, and help them as necessary, and without the work of the booking offices there will be no railway.

Above: Welcome to sunny Minehead! Fortunately passengers approaching the station entrance and the booking office do not usually have these weather conditions to negotiate. The original station booking office was in the centre of the main building, but with this area now given over to administration office space, the current booking office was built by the WSR. The interior incorporates parts of the former booking office at Cardiff General (now Cardiff Central). *Martin Snell*

Left: The interior of a traditional booking office, in this case at Crowcombe Heathfield with the ticket rack containing the 'Edmondson' tickets clearly visible. *Tim Stanger*

Retail and Café staff

Once again most of the stations have some shop and food outlets and volunteer staff to help with the running of these is necessary. The largest Cafés are at Minehead and Bishops Lydeard stations.

Station shops

The two main shops are at Bishops Lydeard and Minehead, but all the stations except Doniford Halt have sales counters. That at Washford specialises in publications relating to the Somerset & Dorset Joint Railway.

The Buffer Stop Shop attracts business both from WSR passengers and from visitors to the town, and the range of goods stocked is aimed at attracting both markets. Book launches and signings, such as that shown here *(above right)* featuring Colin Howard, are a regular part of the calendar. *All WSR Collection*

BY STATION

There are non-alcoholic drinks and sweets available at all stations except Doniford Halt, and Williton also offers sandwiches and ice creams.

Bishops Lydeard

The Whistle Stop Café On Platform 2 adjacent to the signal box, The Whistle Stop Café sells hot and cold snacks as well as a soft drinks and sweets.

Stogumber

Refreshment Room (the old station office) Here you can also partake of one of the station's now famous cream teas. On gala days bacon rolls, sausage rolls and pasties are always popular, and in colder weather tea and crumpets are served.

Minehead

The Turntable Café offers a wide menu including a selection of sandwiches, hot food, chilled items, cakes, biscuits, confectionery and snacks. It also offers a range of freshly made speciality coffees and teas, not forgetting our best-selling mugs of original tea and filter coffee.

Food is fresh and where possible locally sourced. All sandwiches and rolls are freshly made each day. A choice of a fast-track takeaway service or a more leisurely eat-in experience is offered.

Support Groups

As well as all the hands-on work that goes into the year-round story of the WSR there are also a number of support groups which can be joined by those with no ability or wish to be hands-on but who are interested in the railway and its future. Apart from the station "Friends" groups some of the others are as follows:-

The **West Somerset Railway Association** came into being as the plan to reopen the line began to form, and is the longest established support group. It publishes a quarterly magazine to keep members in touch with what is happening on the railway and owns two Great Western Railway steam engines "Small Prairie" tank engine No 4561 *(above right)* and No 7821 *Ditcheat Manor*. At the time of writing the former is being restored in the Williton shed of West Somerset Restorations whilst the "Manor" is at STEAM Museum in Swindon as an exhibit awaiting its turn to be returned to action. West Somerset Restorations is part of the work of the Association, overhauling locomotives and coaches for use on the WSR and also carrying out contract work for other users. There is an apprenticeship scheme as part of the work at Williton which aims to keep traditional crafts skills alive. The Association also runs the shop at Bishops Lydeard station where the administration office can also be found, and another part of the work is ownership and crewing of the "Quantock Belle" dining train. For small groups it is possible to hire an Inspection saloon vehicle for travel, giving excellent all-round views of the countryside along the route.

How to volunteer

Volunteering your time to help the railway:

Individual enquiries and applications are always welcomed at any time. These should be directed to New Volunteer Co-ordinator, c/o The Railway Station, Minehead, TA24 5BG. Telephone 01643 704996 or email: info@wsrail.net

Lots of different skills are required. As a prospective new volunteer you could experience supervised work training in any of the following disciplines:

- Signalman
- Station duties
- Booking Clerk
- Draw tickets
- Retail
- Guard
- Travelling Ticket Inspector (TTI)
- Trackside
- Locomotive
- Locomotive restoration
- Catering
- Publicity
- Permanent way gang
- 'Quantock Belle' dining train
- Restoration and Maintenance Squad (RAMS)
- Signal & Telegraph (S&T)

The West Somerset Steam Railway Trust's purpose is to conserve historical aspects of the WSR and maintain the heritage ambience for future generations. They have a small museum at Blue Anchor station (open on Sundays, Bank Holiday Mondays and during Galas in the main operating season) with the main high-profile work being the "Heritage Carriages Project" which is working on the restoration of historic Great Western Railway vehicles. The first to be restored was an 1897 sleeping car which can usually be viewed in the Gauge Museum at Bishops Lydeard station and work continues on what will be a long-term project at Williton.

The Somerset and Dorset Railway Trust moved to the WSR when their own restoration plans at Radstock collapsed in the mid-1970s. The Radstock Project was on the Somerset and Dorset route between Bath and Bournemouth proper but once it had been undermined by finance and local politics the Trust looked at a number of sites before settling on Washford. They have laid track, having taken over a layout which only had the running line passing the platform, and established a Museum and restoration base. The Trust produces a magazine "Pines Express" which has a mixture of information about SDRT Trust activities and historical articles. The largest individual item which they own is the 7F heavy freight engine No 53808 which works trains on the West Somerset Railway. The small Peckett tank engine *Kilmersdon* gives occasional

Above: Steam locomotives have carried names and numbers right from the start, even if some of the earliest crews would not have been able to read them. These two photographs show part of the interior of Minehead's loco shed with the final fettling up and fitting of Great Western cab-side number plates and name plates for No 6960 *Raveningham Hall. Sam Burton*

Right: 'Push Pull' saloon No 178 at Minehead. *Peter Townsend*

shunting demonstrations in the yard and there is a long-term project to restore former Somerset and Dorset coaches to working order.

Above: The Somerset and Dorset Railway Trust's 7F No 53808 (See page 42) looking resplendent as No 88 in SDJR livery, passing Blue Anchor Beach. *Steve Edge*

The Diesel and Electric Preservation Group were the first into the field of diesel locomotive preservation, recognising in the early 1970s that with the withdrawal of the first-generation main-line diesel locomotive classes by British Rail there was a danger of a part of British railway history being lost. Their first purchase was Class 35 "Hymek" D7017 and as the Group and the collection grew they came to Williton where they have built a depot and a heritage centre where at weekends and galas it is possible for visitors to come and see the achievements for themselves (admission by donation). DEPG locomotives, crewed by members of the group's workforce, operate WSR passenger trains on selected dates during the operating season and there is a successful Driver Experience programme. There is a periodic magazine and a website gives regular news updates.

Friends of the West Somerset Railway is an online-only group which has come into being to fund projects for the West Somerset, starting with improving watering facilities for steam locomotives (which can need refills of up to 4,000 gallons) and in the longer term helping with construction of a permanent locomotive shed at the Bishops Lydeard end of the line.

Amongst the most popular diesel locomotives of the British Railways era were the 'Western' Class diesel-hydraulics. Here is No 1010 *Western Campaigner* at Bishops Lydeard; built in 1962 and withdrawn by BR in 1977, this locomotive is now in the care of the Diesel and Electric Preservation Group. *WSR Collection*

Galas and special events

EXAMPLE EVENTS

Ask for full details, including dates and times, at our Booking Offices.

- Steam Engineman Course
- Diesel Experience Course
- Snow Drops and Steam
- Spring Steam Gala
- 'The Quantock Belle' 1st Class Dining Train
- 'Dunster Castle Express'
- Exmoor Day Out by Steam Train and Classic Coach
- 'Hestercombe Express'
- Murder Mystery Specials
- Mixed Traction Weekend
- Day Out With Thomas™
- Fish and Chip Special
- Cheese and Cider Specials
- Steam and Cream Special
- Steam Fayre and Vintage Vehicle Rally
- Late Summer Weekend
- Autumn Steam Gala
- Santa Express and Santa Specials
- Dunster By Candlelight
- Carol Trains
- Winter Steam Festival

THEMED TRAINS

The core of the railway's business is its 200-days-a-year train operation, but this is augmented by special workings for those who are looking for something "extra" or just a little different. "Murder Mystery" trains offer a chance to exercise the 'little grey cells' to solve the murder resulting from the scenes played out before you on the journey. Fish and Chip Specials, Steam and Cream, and Cider and Cheese are also popular parts of the annual programme.

Other popular packages include the Lynton and Lynmouth Explorer and the Watchet Afternoon Explorer. The railway also operates bus links from Dunster station for the annual Country Fair and Dunster Show days.

SANTA SPECIALS

The Santa trains run at weekends and other selected dates from early December up to and including Christmas Eve. "Santa Expresses" operate from Bishops Lydeard and Minehead, with Santa walking through the train with his helpers, while 'Santa Specials' run from Bishops Lydeard and Minehead to visit the man in the red suit at his grottos at Crowcombe Heathfield and Blue Anchor. The fares include the train journey, a present for each child and some seasonal refreshments for the adults.

Right: A model poses on the platform at Crowcombe Heathfield during a professional 'shoot'; actors perform aboard a Murder Mystery train, with a passenger dressing for the part; and a flyer for the dastardly deeds ahead on the annual Christmas Murder Mystery. *Tim Stanger/Jacquie Green*

GALAS

The West Somerset Railway's Gala events are a popular part of the annual diary for many enthusiasts and also a great day out for the general public who want to see a wide selection of locomotives in action.

The Spring Steam Gala is one of the major events of its kind and has grown to the point where it takes place over the last two weekends of March (barring an early Easter), with the second weekend also incorporating the preceding Thursday and Friday. Apart from benefiting the railway, this Gala also brings welcome early-season trade to many local accommodation providers.

The Mixed Traffic Weekend is three days when the WSR works virtually all of its trains using vintage diesel locomotives, many being from the DEPG collection at Williton, and with the diesel-hydraulic machines of the former Western Region of British Railways very evident. This Gala usually takes place in mid-June.

The Autumn Steam Gala is a four-day event that takes place at the juncture of September and October, and is another major treat for all lovers of the steam locomotive.

All three of these major events feature trade stands and other attractions to augment the intensive train services, and "guest" locomotives are hired from other heritage railways to augment the home-based fleets.

Above: Steam locomotives at the servicing area at Bishops Lydeard are ready for duty on a day with 'Santa Express' and 'Santa Special' operations taking place. *Alan Meade*

Below: An on-train buffet car volunteer suitably attired looks out of the window before a 'Santa' train leaves Bishops Lydeard, while on board a 'Santa Express' a young passenger seems pleased to meet the man in the red suit during his annual visit to the WSR. *Sam Burton*

The Late Summer Weekend takes place on the first weekend in September and features a mixture of steam and vintage diesel locomotives, mostly drawn from the home fleet but with some guest appearances taking place. Similarly, the Winter Steam Festival, which takes place on two days between Christmas and New Year, is mainly concerned with WSR-based engines, but a guest does appear from time to time.

Above: This panoramic view shows the curve of Blue Anchor Bay looking towards Blue Anchor station and the railway following the coastline to Dunster and Minehead. The up train leaving the station is about to start the climb inland towards Washford, which includes the steepest gradient on the WSR, a section at 1 in 65. *WSR Collection*

Below: The headboard of the twice-weekly 'Dunster Castle Express' train incorporates the logo of the National Trust, in whose care the castle now is. *Steve Guscott*

Below right: No 9351 has the 900-years-older castle at Dunster as a backdrop while making its way towards Minehead with a down train. The castle sits on its hill above the attractive medieval village, which is around 20 minutes walking time from the station. *Steve Guscott*

THEMED TRIPS TO LOCAL ATTRACTIONS

The West Somerset is increasingly working to offer 'more than a train ride', with additional packages on selected dates. There is the 'Dunster Castle Express' twice a week from Bishops Lydeard with a coach link from Dunster station to the Castle for a day out at this 1,000-year-old part of British history. Running on selected dates from the Minehead end of the line, the 'Hestercombe Express' has a coach link to these wonderfully restored formal gardens.

Other popular packages include a steam train ride combined with a 'Mystery Tour' by coach around Exmoor, a day out by train and coach exploring the remains of the West Somerset Mineral Railway, and a new link to visit the Exmoor Pony Centre. The railway also operates bus links from Dunster station for the annual Country Fair and Dunster Show days.